Peafowl

Victoria Blakemore

vblakemore.author@gmail.com

Copyright info/picture credits

Cover, allanlau2000/Pixabay; Page 3, rycky21/Pixabay; Page 5, EdwinSurbeck/Pixabay; Page 7, Prashe/Pixabay; Page 9, DanielAlon/Pixabay; Page 11, Katja/AdobeStock; Pages 12-13, Storyblocks; Page 15, Rido7/Pixabay; Page 17, Pexels/Pixabay; Page 19, sapgreen/AdobeStock; Page 21, TheUjulala/Pixabay; Page 23; Capri23auto/Pixabay; Page 25, selene2303/Pixabay; Page 27, Kari_Izq/Pixabay; Page 29, Alexas_Fotos/Pixabay; Page 31, alexmleite/Pixabay; Page 33, allanlau2000/Pixabay

Table of Contents

What Are Peafowl?

Peafowl are large birds. Although they are often called peacocks, the word peacock is actually a male bird. Peafowl is the name for the male and female birds.

There are three kinds of peafowl. They differ in color and where they live.

The Indian peacock is the most

well-known kind of peafowl.

Peafowl are one of the largest birds that can fly. Adults usually weigh between eight and thirteen pounds.

Males can be up to 7.5 feet long. More than half of that can be their train of feathers.

Physical Characteristics

Peafowl have a crest of feathers on their head. They are small feathers with round ends.

Peacocks are known for their long train of feathers. The train covers the tail feathers that are below.

The feathers of a peacock's

train have round parts called

eyes or ocelli.

White Peafowl

White peafowl are Indian peafowl that hatch with white feathers.

They are usually found in **captivity**. They are not common in the wild, but are sometimes found in parts of India.

Some people think that white peafowl are **albinos**. They are not. Their feathers are white, but their eyes are still blue.

9

Habitat

Peafowl are able to **adapt** to living in many habitats. They are often found in forests, grasslands, and rainforests.

In forests and rainforests, peafowl often **roost** in the trees. This helps to keep them safe from **predators**.

Peafowl are found on the
continents of Africa, Asia, and
Australia.

They are often seen in India,

China, Myanmar, and Sri Lanka.

Peafowl are **omnivores**. This means that they eat meat and plants.

Their diet is made up of fruit, leaves, seeds, insects, small mammals, and rodents. They are not usually **picky** about what they eat.

Peafowl often **forage** for food in the morning and late evening. The temperature is cooler then.

15

Communication

Peafowl use sound and movement to communicate with each other.

Peacocks fan and flutter their train feathers. They also make sounds with their tails that are too low for humans to hear.

Peafowl have a very loud call that they make. They are often heard in the morning and evening.

Movement

Peafowl have strong legs. They are able to run up to ten miles per hour.

They also use their legs if they are in danger. They have a sharp spur on the back of their leg. It can be used to kick predators.

Although peafowl can fly, their

wingspan is small for birds of

their size. They cannot fly for

long distances.

Peacocks

Peacocks are male peafowl. They are almost twice the size of female peafowl.

Peacock feathers are different from most other bird feathers. They have a special crystal-like feature that make them shimmer in the light.

Peacocks fan their train of feathers out to **attract** a peahen. They also fan it if they feel **threatened**.

21

Peahens

Peahens are female peafowl.

They are usually brown,

beige, and cream in color.

Indian peahens do not have

a long train of feathers like

peacocks. Green peahens

have a short train of feathers.

Some peahens may have

some blue or green feathers

on their neck.

Peachicks

Peahens scratch a hole in the dirt and cover it with sticks. Then, they lay up to eight eggs and sit on them to **incubate** them. The eggs hatch after about four weeks.

When they first hatch, peachicks have brown feathers.

Peachicks are unable to fly for the first two weeks. Their mother stays close to keep them safe.

Peafowl Life

Peafowl are often found in groups. These groups are called ostentations, parties, or musters. They often forage for food together.

Peafowl often preen their feathers by picking at them with their beaks. This keeps them clean and looking good.

In the wild, peafowl can live about twenty years. They may live longer in **captivity** where they are safe from predators.

Population

Researchers are not sure how many peafowl there are in the wild. They are very common in many places.

The Indian peafowl is thought to be **stable** in the wild. They are not in danger of becoming **extinct**.

Green peafowl populations have been **declining**. They are often hunted for their meat. They are also caught and sold as pets.

Helping Peafowl

Indian peafowl are doing well in the wild. They do not need help to survive.

China now has laws that protect green peafowl from being hunted. People are also trying to protect the habitats of green peafowl so they have a safe place to live.

When people have peafowl as pets, they can get lost. The birds may also need a new home if people move.

There are groups that help people who lose their peafowl or need a new home for their peafowl. They want the birds to have a safe home.

Glossary

Adapt: to change

Albino: a plant, animal, or human born without normal coloration

Attract: to get the attention of

Captivity: when animals are kept by humans

Declining: getting smaller

Extinct: when there are no more of an animal left in the wild

Forage: to look for food

Incubate: keeping eggs warm until they

hatch

Omnivore: an animal that eats meat and plants

Picky: hard to please

Predators: animals that hunt other animals for food

Roost: a perch that birds may sleep or rest on

Stable: steady, staying the same

Threatened: in danger

Territory: an area of land that an animal claims as its own

Wingspan: the length of a bird's wings from tip to tip

Victoria Blakemore is a first grade

teacher in Southwest Florida with a

passion for reading.

You can visit her at

www.elementaryexplorers.com

Also in This Series

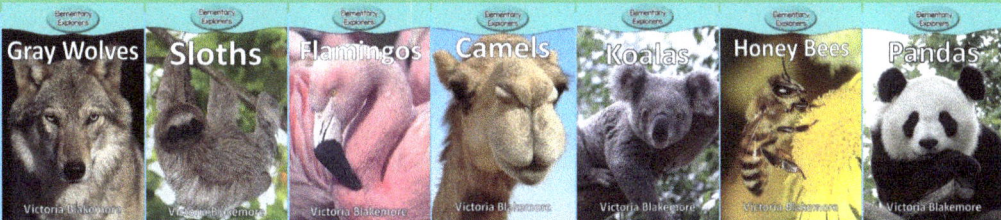

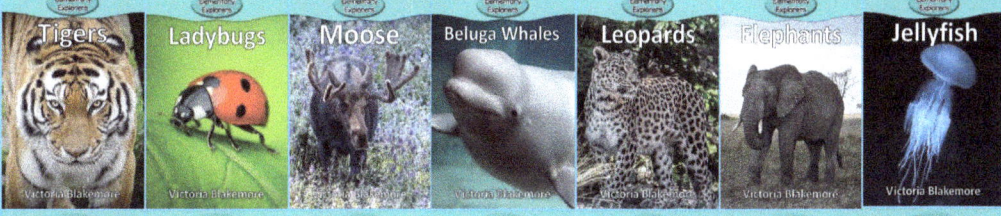

Gray Wolves	Sloths	Flamingos	Camels	Koalas	Honey Bees	Pandas
Pangolins	White-Tailed Deer	Orcas	Giraffes	Corn	Meerkats	Echidnas
Walruses	Raccoons	Bald Eagles	Apples	Arctic Foxes	Red Pandas	Cassowaries
Tigers	Ladybugs	Moose	Beluga Whales	Leopards	Elephants	Jellyfish
Binturongs	Lions	Dolphins	Reindeer	Hammerhead Sharks	Hippos	Pumpkins
Peafowl	Chameleons	Florida Panthers	Aye-Ayes	Black Bears	Cheetahs	Manatees
Gingerbread	Polar Bears	Hot Chocolate	Orangutans	Coyotes	Marshmallows	Strawberries

Also in This Series

Aardvarks	Mako Sharks	Alligators	Frogs	Hedgehogs	Brown Bears	Bongos
Sea Turtles	Quokkas	Muskrats	Zebras	Red Foxes	Ring-Tailed Lemurs	Platypuses
Anteaters	Kangaroos	Rhinos	Jaguars	Wombats	Capybaras	Gorillas
Cats	Skunks	Butterflies	Dingoes	Snow Leopards	African Wild Dogs	Penguins
Whale Sharks	Wolverines	Warthogs	Caracals	Badgers	Seals	Hummingbirds
Pikas	Humpback Whales	Pumas	Lemonade	Llamas	Tulips	Ostriches
Sunflowers	Fennec Foxes	Sea Lions				

Victoria Blakemore

www.ingramcontent.com/pod-product-compliance
Lightning Source LLC
Chambersburg PA
CBHW051253020426
42333CB00025B/3183